LANDMARK COLLECTOR'S LIBRARY

THE SPIRIT OF DUFFIELD

THE 20TH CENTURY IN PHOTOGRAPHS

Derek Wigley

LANDMARK COLLECTOR'S LIBRARY

THE SPIRIT OF
DUFFIELD
THE 20TH CENTURY IN PHOTOGRAPHS

Derek Wigley

Landmark Publishing

Published by

Landmark Publishing Ltd
Ashbourne Hall, Cokayne Ave, Ashbourne, Derbyshire DE6 1EJ England
Tel: (01335) 347349 Fax: (01335) 347303
e-mail: landmark@clara.net
web site: www.landmarkpublishing.co.uk

ISBN 1 84306 066 3

British Library Cataloguing in Publication Data: a catalogue
record for this book is available from the British Library.

Print: Bookcraft, Midsomer Norton
Design: Mark Titterton
Cover: James Allsopp

Front cover: Cottages in Hazelwood Road; **Back cover top:** Duffield Church Sunday School in the early
1950s; **Middle:** Ecclesbourne Upper VIth form May Leavers Ball, 1993; **Bottom:** Duffield Bank Railway,
Tennis Court Station; **Title page:** Boating on the Derwent, 1920s.

CONTENTS

Acknowledgements

The invitation to compile a pictorial record of Duffield in the 20th century carried with it the brief that it should primarily be of its people and their activity. Requests for contributions met with enthusiastic response, and more material was offered than can actually be included in this book. Unfortunately there are blanks in some areas because events have not been photographically recorded, hence cannot be reproduced. The range of topics included is, however, extremely wide, and it seems reasonable to suppose that, through these records, "The Spirit of Duffield" may be perceived. Acknowledgements are gratefully extended as follows:

To Marion Taulbut, who suggested that I undertake the task, contributing photos of St Alkmund's Church and its congregation plus other facets of the village with contributions from Philip Radford, T. Alton, N. Pooley and James Bell. To Derbyshire County Council's Libraries with particular thanks to Ruth Gordon of the Local Studies Library and Heritage Department and Ruth Sharpe of the Duffield Branch Library for the use of items in the Bromby Collection. To John Cash for items from the archives of the Duffield Branch of the Royal British Legion plus items from his personal collection. To Derby Daily Telegraph for permission to reproduce photos of the British Legion, Carnival Queen and Dedication at William Gilbert's School. To Adrian Farmer and the Belper News for pictures and the use of their records. To Derrick Lodge for some fine examples of Duffield's Scout and Guide activity, and other subjects. To Duffield Women's Institute for the use of their records to illustrate the extent of their activity over 80 years. To Miss Joan Hingley for supplying photographs of A. Hingley, Timber Merchants. To Cumberhills W.I. and Sandra Dare for materials showing activity and expertise extending far beyond the parish boundaries. To 620 (Duffield) Sqn. A.T.C. with Ian Cowley for some fine examples from the records of Duffield's Air Cadets. To Tony Gray for photos of Duffield Service Station and surroundings. To Derek Cook and Duffield Community Association for material which reflects many aspects of village life. D.C.A.'s activity extends far beyond the records shown here. Decorations and plantings, litter picks, Neighbourhood Watch, Quizes and the Carnival and associated activity. To Dr J. Robert Dupey and the Ecclesbourne School for material which exhibits social as well as academic activity plus involvement with the community. To John Reece and William Gilbert's School for an insight into its long history and achievement. To Rex Bleakman and Meadows Primary School for some great examples of "children doing things". To Mrs J. Bonsall for some early views of the village. To Mike Stanier and Derwent Valley Wind Band whose membership includes whole families and players of all abilities. To David Thorn for material from Duffield Cricket Club covering the whole of the century, plus activity in Duffield Club, also enthusiastic advice. To Duffield Bellringers and Katy Todd for items giving some insight into the world of campanology. To Duffield Tennis Club for a view of their facility. To Winifred Silver and Duffield Flower Group for pictures of some fine displays viewed in many locations. To Mr J. Cooper for his help in identifying members of the Duffield Church Choir.

Foreword

From the early 17th century Duffield had been recognised by discerning citizens as a good place to live. Away from hazards normally associated with town life, it offered a genteel approach to country living within an independently minded community.

The movement was gradual until improved travelling was offered by Turnpike roads, and a century later by the railways, a number of whose Company employees also took up residence. Architect-designed Georgian houses were joined, mainly at at the village's extremities, by substantial and elegant Victorian edifices.

The village was agricultural, surrounded by 18 farms, with specialist horse breeding augmenting arable and dairy farming. The village was self-sustaining and self-contained, with a surplus of produce to sell in outside markets. Twice yearly cattle and horse fairs were also held along the Town Street.

At the beginning of the 20th century, besides farmers, there were 5 framework knitters, 5 butchers, 7 grocers, 2 coal merchants, cornmills, forges and a malthouse plus a quarry and 6 public houses. During the 20th century the village changed dramatically. The population increased by more than double.

A number of organisations founded in the 19th century remained and grew. Some of them celebrated their first centenaries. These included Duffield Cricket Club, the Duffield Bellringers, the Parish Council and Duffield Club, also the Derbyshire Building Society which made Duffield Hall its headquarters soon after St Ronan's School, established after the first World War, closed. Trinity Methodist Church is approaching its centenary although the movement extends much further.

Evidence of independent thought extends over centuries. Nonconformity was evident in the registration, by Thomas Newton, of his recently built house (Duffield Hall) as a meeting house of Dissenters during the Commonwealth. By 1800 there were three chapels besides the Parish Church which served a very large area, greater even that the original Frith now extant as Duffield Deanery.

Farming remains, although different in operation. Horsebreeding has only diminished, with horsepower now largely provided by the internal combustion engine. A brief flirtation with motorised transport was seen with MacEvoy's motor cycles. Methods of ploughing and harvesting have been updated by more versatile machines, mainly in the last two decades. During World War II hitherto unploughed fields were planted with sugar-beet.

Railway freight services disappeared and passenger services reduced. The colour works, which came to the village in the 19th century, has relocated, as has the sawmill and timberyard, away from the village altogether. Milford Mills who drew some workers from Duffield, either as hands or outworkers, closed and the several retail outlets much reduced.

The number of houses has increased dramatically. Initially there was steady ribbon development, but in the 1950's Hall Farm, New Zealand Farm and a large part of Cumberhills Farm were given over to housing. A number of crofts and smallholdings and part of Duffield Park went for housing and schools.

The creation of the Ecclesbourne School, which soon acquired a strong academic reputation, accelerated growth. William Gilbert's School, moved gradually through several sites finally consolidating in 1992. A new additional Primary School, Duffield Meadows, was also founded.

Several associations have functioned for much of the century, these include Scouts and Guides and Duffield W.I. with the British Legion and later the D.C.A. offering community activity for the greater part of it.

A second W.I., Cumberhills, was formed in the early 60s with many of its members being newcomers to the village. Their meetings were held in the evenings while Duffield W.I. met in the afternoons. Both had a wide range of activities from home economics, crafts, drama and choir as well as social functions.

Continued infilling, proposed development and service requirements created by expansion have, at times, caused grave concern for parish council and residents. The floodings in the 1920s and 30s may have been brought about by repairs to the sluice gates at Peckwash Mill, raising the river level in 1918 by 18". Prior to this, to augment power from the five water wheels, the owner had added an engine and large chimney. The smoke created was considered to be a nuisance and injunctions were sought and obtained to apply when smoke approached Eaton Bank. During severe flooding in the 60s the weir collapsed. Extensive flood prevention works were applied to the River Ecclesbourne soon afterwards. The problem still exists. It is a very old one, referred to in a document of 1159.

Withdrawals of services, or threats of them, have met with protests in various forms. The cessation of stopping mainline trains at Duffield Station was followed by a proposal to withdraw passenger services altogether. After strong protest railcars continue in service. A recent proposal, which is welcomed, is of services to run on the Wirksworth line.

Closure of the Midland (now HSBC) and NatWest Bank branches have successfully been resisted. The closure of the Branch Library for two years was fought by letter, through the press, T.V. and at meetings. The strongest protests concerned the Ecclesbourne School, firstly for the retaining of the VIth form and then with 'Opting Out'. These campaigns touched County Hall and the House of Commons.

Planning proposals have occasionally resulted in very large attendances at Parish Council meetings, and in 1991 the Annual Parish Meeting, at the Meadows School, resulted in 'standing room only' when a proposal for a link road from Wirksworth Road to the Colour Works with associated housing, was put forward.

The Millennium was marked with events and artefacts. A Time Capsule and Millennium Milepost were placed on Wirksworth Road corner. A banner showing many village scenes has been widely exhibited. 14 acres of Eyes Meadow have been planted to regenerate wildlife in a "Millennium Meadow".

Village life goes on. The majority of the pictures shown here have not been published previously, and acknowledgement of the private collections is given separately. Collectively they present a unique view of the village and its residents, through which, it is hoped, "The Spirit of Duffield" may be perceived.

(Above) This opening picture encapsulates the features from which "The Spirit of Duffield" in the 20th century is evoked. Trees abound; but this is only a small part of an ancient wood, fifty kilometres in circumference, named Duffield Frith. The River Derwent is a scenic river but viewed with awe when in flood. Ancient tracks cross the scene together with roads developed from the 16th century. St Alkmund's Church was founded in the 9th century and just beyond were the Saxon, Danish and early Norman villages. The railway had a great influence on residential growth. *(Below)* The Bridge Inn. Originally named "The Bull's Head" this is how it appeared early in the century.

(Top) Duffield Hall. The main building, dating from the 1630s, had additions made in the 19th century by Rowland Smith whose family owned it until 1919.

(Above left) In the Duffield Hall Grounds.

(Above right) The Hall and Tennis Court.

(Right) Hall Farm. The main buildings on Wirksworth Road were demolished when the area was put to residential development in the 1950s.

(Above left) The Old Vicarage. This vicarage replaced one in the churchyard. It was situated in extensive grounds, now built on. It stood for barely a century.

(Above right) The Mill on Snake Lane. The Ecclesbourne River provided the power for three mills in Duffield from the time of the Norman conquest. That nearest the village was called 'papermill'. Demolished in 1961.

One of a number of bridges over the river, although the main crossings were by ford. The lowest of the three watermills stood on Duck Island, to the right of the picture. The houses are in Tamworth Street.

This mill, sometimes referred to as Domesday Mill because it was there at the time of the survey (1086), was built by Fulcher, one of Henry de Ferrers "lieutenants". The family were mill wrights; they lived at Ireton (between Duffield and Kedleston) building a number of mills. In 1330 they were granted Champeyne Park at Cumberhills as part of their estate, and taken out of the Duffield Forest's administration.

Hazelwood Road. This shows part of the oldest road in Duffield. Pictured on the left is the entrance to "The Glen"; at the lower end of its ground were brickworks. The sign of the New Inn is just visible and beyond is the entrance to the cemetery. Sharpening stones for scythes were once quarried in the immediate area.

(Above) View from the Meadow. The path crossing Parsons and Wall Croft Meadow was once the main way into Town Street. The horses were an even more familiar sight at the beginning of the century. *(Below)* Georgian and Victorian Town Street.

The White Hart, Duffield's coaching Inn, with small forge at the rear. An important social centre for the village where meetings and the occasional concert took place. Demolished in the late 30s it was replaced with the present, more spacious, building. For some years the neighbouring shop (now Duffield News) served as the Post Office.

Town Street and Wirksworth Road corner. This view shows the old White Hart and some nearby shops. Included also is part of the front garden of "The Hollies" where "The Village Store" now stands. Beside Gervase House was the former Co-op shop, a cottage with another, named "The Powder Room" just out of sight. This was where gunpowder was stored during the Napoleonic wars.

(Above) The Old Forge. Facing Wirksworth Road the Forge, also a whitesmith, continued to function long after World War II. The smith's name was Abell. The residential part remains. *(Below)* The Old School House. This stood in King Street. With changes to William Gilbert's School it was vacated and became the 'Parish Room'. Demolished in 1963, a bungalow now occupies the site.

(Above) The Station. Once a hive of activity with wharves adjacent on the Wirksworth line. There was a newspaper stall on the station, with a footbridge on to Eyes Meadow. (Below) Postern Terrace. This view from King Street looking into Town Street shows two wagons, one at least delivering coal.

(Above) King Street. This early picture gives little sign of future traffic. Note Trinity Methodist Church, completed in October 1904. *(Below)* Cottages in Hazelwood Road. This elegant scene shows cottages adjacent to Phillips Croft. The gates at which the lady stands are still in position although the tops of the stone gate posts are no longer to be seen.

(Above) Duffield Bank Railway. Sir Arthur Percival Heywood, engineer (and philanthropist), built a figure-of-eight track in the grounds of "Springwood". The track is now gone although an engine still survives (in Wales). *(Below)* Tennis Court Station.

(Above) The Viaduct. Another scenic section of Duffield Bank Railway. *(Below)* Duffield Bank Railway was a complete system for goods as well as passengers; pictured here is a parcel van.

(Above) Old cottages in Tamworth Street. *(Below)* The Kings Head. A survey of 1568 records six inns or alehouses in Duffield. This must be a direct descendant of one of these. It was situated where Town Street branched. The main route led to Hazelwood (and Wirksworth) and the other, with a riverside path to Milford, and a track through Ford's Mouth Close to a ford across the Derwent. This led to Makeney and Holbrook. This route, after the creation of the Chesterfield turnpike road, became known as 'Save Penny Lane'.

(Above) Duffield Art Gallery and Antiques. This was a shoe shop in the early part of the century. Visible to the rear is a former framework knitter's cottage. *(Below)* Framework Knitter's Cottage.

(Above) Commandeering of Horses. During World War I, with little mechanisation, horses were needed on 'The Front'. This is one of several pictures recording the commandeering taking place on Castle Hill.

(Left) The Masonic Hall. Ecclesbourne Lodge 2425 was created in 1892 with meetings held at the White Hart until 1904 when this former Wesleyan chapel in King Street was purchased. Alterations made to the building included a new fascia. Several Lodges now meet there.

(Right) The gasworks, plus retort were built in the 1860s to supply gas to Quarndon, Allestree and Duffield. A few gas lamps can still be seen around Duffield. Early street lighting was by oil lamp. The works ceased to operate in 1930.

(Above) Hawley's Colour Works. This view from Cork Hill shows the Colour Works which came here in the 19th century. (Below) Cumberhills Farm. Houses now occupy much of the former farmland. The 1881 Ordnance Survey map named it "Promised Land Farm".

(Left) October 1930. Brothers Frank, Alf and Albert Ford, moving timber from Allestree Hill below Evans Avenue for road widening on the A6.

(Below) April 1946. The first consignment of German Spruce, felled by the British Army of occupation, to arrive in the yard of A. Hingley, Timber Merchants of Duffield. 100 tons in the picture will be used for housing. Metal detectors had to be used on the trees before sawing as some contained shrapnel and bullets which would rip the teeth off the saws. In the background can be seen the Milford Road Railway Bridge carrying the A6 to Belper. Behind are the Chevin Golf Links.

(Above and below) A Ploughing Match being viewed by pupils of Meadows Primary School.

Chapter 2 – The Derwent

The convergence of a prehistoric trackway descending from the Pennine hills with the River Derwent, "flowing through the oak trees", may explain Duffield's origins. The river itself, with many changes in depth and water level, liable to sudden floods and treacherous currents was less suitable for transportation than some other rivers. The Trent was well used, but the gravelly shallows at Derwent Mouth probably precluded all but occasional use. It was probably limited to small boats over comparatively short distances.

The use of a barge to carry firewood from Belper to Darley Abbey was recorded in one of the Earl of Derby's charters (1159). The construction of weir and sluice gates at Darley in 1220 would have restricted further movement. Similar construction at Peckwash in 1425 would have caused further restriction. Fords at Thornlea (near Allestree), Duffield and approaching Milford may well have restricted river use to fishing which was strictly controlled.

At the beginning of the 20th century there was pleasure boating on a $1^{3}/_{4}$ mile reach between Milford and Peckwash based on landing stages at Derwent Cottage tea rooms and the Bridge Inn. Towards the end of World War I, John Briggs of Town Street was preparing a detailed survey of this section and in 1917 he produced a book of plans, depth charts, sketches and photographs, noting all hazards. With a descriptive text there were details of four of the boats. These were "Olive" and "Hebe", a double sculled skiff, to which were added "Nancy", a Nottingham built boat launched on Whit Tuesday 1921, and "Bessie", Burton built and launched on June 29, 1921, the day of King George V's visit to the Royal Show in Derby.

The original work is in the Bromby Local History Collection in Duffield Library.

(Above) Boating on the Derwent, a popular activity in the early 1900s.

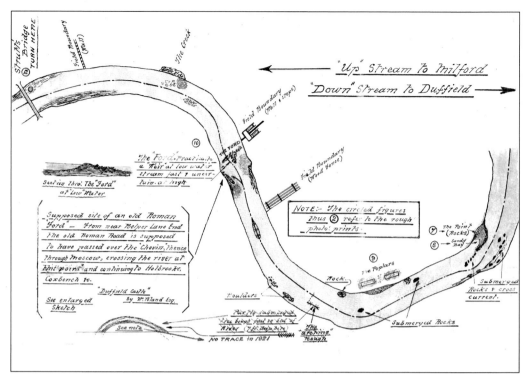

John Briggs' plans of the Derwent.

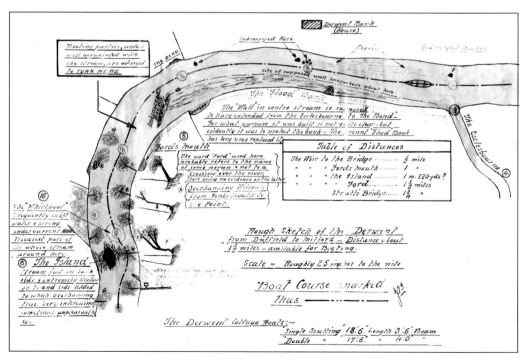

A Single Sculled Boat.

View from the bridge.

(Above) A canvas canoe. *(Below)* At Derwent Cottage landing.

(Above) "The Island". *(Below)* Derwent Bank house in John Briggs' text, now Rolls-Royce Guest House, "Duffield Bank House".

(Above) At Derwent Cottage landing. *(Below)* Fishing on the Derwent.

(Above) Churchyard riverside walk. *(Below)* Above the landing stage.

(Above) Strutts Bridge. *(Below)* Ford's Mouth from the northern bank.

(Above) "Olive" in Sandy Bay. (Below) The Weir at Peckwash Mill. Repairs to the sluices in 1918 raised the river level by 18 inches.

Chapter 3 – Around the Village

The 19th century saw major changes to the village roads. Tamworth Street, in earlier days, passed around the Park, also led to the three water mills and was named "Back Street". In two stages a new turnpike road to Wirksworth was created (1808), also laying out a new section from Hall Farm to the Toll House. The roads leading to the ford across the Derwent, with branch to Milford, had passed in front of "The King's Head". This was blocked off and "New Road" constructed with a bridge across the Ecclesbourne. With the building of a new Wesleyan chapel it was renamed Chapel Street.

Major changes took place because of the railways. Castle Orchard was divided by the cutting of a road into the castle mound, to use a bridge rather than a level crossing on the main line. The Wirksworth line required changes including the making of Milford Road, plus changes in King Street. Castle Hill was built before the end of the century and Avenue Road a few years later.

The 20th century saw Broadway, first as a superior housing development, expanded and converted into a main through road with major infilling between it and the River Ecclesbourne. This section gives a brief indication of the expansion and infrastructure in the village.

(Above) From Castle Mound. The scene towards Milford showing the mainline railway, Milford Mills, the A6, Moscow Farm and Lower Chevin. The area in the immediate foreground was named "Castle Orchard" in the Enclosure Award, beyond which were the castle fishponds.

(Left) Flaxholme from Bunkers Hill. Burley Meadows is in the foreground and Peckwash Mill near the centre.

(Left) Peckwash Chimney. The history of Peckwash dates from 1425. From 1794 its water courses also fed the Derby Canal. The use of the chimney was beset by litigation early in the 20th century. The weir was raised in 1917 and damaged by flooding in the 1960s.

(Below) The Beach. A pastoral scene below Peckwash weir.

(Above) Burley Hill Farm. Before 1756 the road to Duffield Bridge passed this way. The alternative route was via Allestree Common and Burley Lane. Heavy draught shire-horses were bred here, particularly sought after by breweries. *(Below)* These fine dray-horses, similar to those bred by the Appleby family, were seen at Duffield Carnival in 1997.

(Above) The Church Hall pictured here during the First World War when it was used as a convalescent hospital for soldiers, seen here with the Red Cross flag proudly flying.

(Right) The Hall today which was converted to a private dwelling in 1992.

(Left) Church and Memorial. The War Memorial was placed on land bought from the Railway and dedicated in 1921. Originally the fenced area was grassed.

(Right) Radfords Garage on Town Street, in the 1950s. Six garages operated in Duffield during the century. This view also shows Sloan's shop at the entrance to Chapel Street. The Garage premises have been converted to Mews housing.

(Left) The first Pat Smith shop. Redevelopment of Town Street's retail facilities took place in the 1970s.

Grocers, butchers, greengrocers and other trades, Mac's Electrics, Peta Jordan Boutique, fabrics and haberdashery and newsagents were joined by new enterprises including this one for baby and children's clothes. A high class ladies fashion shop, adjacent to a new post office, followed.

(Below) This view shows Flaxholme Garage (now replaced) and the Council Depot.

(*Above*) Adjacent to the bridges across the Ecclesbourne are Duffield Club's premises, with bank below. The clock commemorates the Club's centenary. (*Below*) New Bridge Inn. In the 1930s both Bridge Inn and White Hart were replaced with new buildings.

(Above) Duffield Post Office in the late 1950s was adjoining Duffield House. This was replaced by a three storey building with doctors' surgeries on the ground floor.

(Left) An early morning view of Town Street and Postern Terrace with Percy Taylor delivering the morning 'pinta'.

(Above) Old Broadway. A late 1950s view. New development was starting. The old malthouse was still standing. At the beginning of the century furniture (including coffins) was built there.

(Above) New Zealand Lane. This shows the junction of Hall Farm Road and the rear of houses on Broadway — part of the great expansion of the village's houses.

(Right) Partly completed New Zealand Lane and the site of Duffield Service Station.

(Below) Duffield Service Station. By the end of the century the only supplier of fuel in the village.

(Above) A Later View of the canopied forecourt of Tony Gray's premises. *(Below)* Adjacent Shops. The area development was associated with the creation of the Ecclesbourne School and an additional Primary School, The Meadows, built in 1965. It included shops and a public house, almost creating two adjacent villages with some common facilities.

(Above) The Scarsdale. As first built, and in addition to the White Hart, King's Head, New Inn, Patten Makers Arms and Bridge Inn. The official opening was carried out by Lord Scarsdale and later renamed, Lord Scarsdale. (Below) The withdrawal of stopping main-line passenger trains saw the removal of the station buildings and footbridge to Eyes Meadow. A railcar service remained after very strong representations.

These two pictures show restoration work to the timbers caused by beetle problems in the roof of St Alkmund's Church in 1963. Pictured is Mr Rowley-Brooke of Timber Decay Remedial Services Ltd.

(Left) Duffield Hall. Following the closure of St Ronan's School the Hall's future was uncertain. Screened by a wall, little was visible from the outside. Seen here is the Hall, with wall removed, as the frontage of the Derbyshire Building Society's H.Q. In the meadow foreground are hollow ways and house platforms of part of the Norman village.

(Left) The DBS Balloon. As the century progressed ballooning increased in popularity, although microlights and paragliding are evidently also on the increase.

(Below) Aerial view of The Derbyshire Building Society's new headquarters. These opened in November 1977.

(Above) Aerial view of The Derbyshire Building Society with new houses in St Ronan's Avenue, also shown are the old people's bungalows in Ecclesbourne Close. *(Below)* The former Midland Bank, this is now the HSBC Bank. A greengrocer's shop stood at the side, later the "Gallery Restaurant". Duffield's first brick kilns stood on the ground behind, later cut out for the laying of the Wirksworth Branch railway.

(*Above*) Duffield Library and reading rooms had several locations in the village including the former Unitarian Chapel and Parish Room. The present library was built, to an award winning design, in 1964. (*Below*) Sunlight Laundry. For many years these premises adjacent to Flaxhome Farm served a wide area as the Cavendish Laundry. Currently, as Sunlight, it is part of a national service in workwear, linen and dust control mats.

(Above and below) Two pictures by Nigel Pooley show the installation of a new footbridge across the Wirksworth Line in March 1979. The line was in use for a further 7 years.

(Below) The last passenger train on the Wirksworth Line in spring 1986. Current proposals are in hand to restore services on this line.

(Above) In 1990 a decision was made to build a new parish hall, adjacent to St Alkmund's Church. The building committee are seen here in the churchyard. The Rev. Arthur Geary-Stevens, Duncan Fish, Dr James Mason, Anthony Rossi, Derek Smith, Frank Troughton and Graham Newton.

(Below) The contractor, Peter Baines, with the architect, Anthony Rossi.

(*Above*) Work under way in 1991. (*Below*) The opening of the new hall in 1992 by the Bishop of Derby, the Rt Rev. Peter Dawes. Also in the picture are members of the choir, the Vicar, Mrs Dawes, local clergy and lay readers.

Duffield's first Dissenters meeting house was the Unitarian Chapel. Later additions disguised the square shape, typical of many Derbyshire Chapels. It served many functions after its religious use ended. At different times in this century it was a school, a reading room, engineering works and the home of Abbeydale pottery. A block of apartments now occupies the site.

(Above) Percy Taylor gave 36 years service to his milk round. He also served on the Parish Council for 16 years, including a term in the 'chair'. *(Below)* Appletree Medical Centre. During the century medical practices had, at different times, operated from Gervase House, Old Walls, The Gables, Duffield House and Ecciesbourne Avenue Surgery. The last two practices were combined in 1994 as the "Appletree Medical Practice". A new centre was built and opened in 1999. "Friends of Appletree Medical Centre" raised a considerable sum of money to assist its work.

Chapter 4 – Dangers and Defences

Many different hazards affected village life over the centuries. There have been reactions to several including road usage and accidents occurring. Infectious diseases briefly produced an isolation hospital, but Duffield's most serious recurrent problem of the century must be flooding.

The low-lying nature of the early village suggests that this may not always have been so. The 17th century Cumberhills drain was cut for a major purpose, since public works are rare. Shown here are some records of the events of the 20s, 30s and 60s and the relief scheme carried out on the River Ecclesbourne. Also shown, in light hearted mood, is Duffield's Fire Service, for whose services we are very grateful.

(Above and right) Two views from Bunkers Hill. These scenes sparked off the flood relief work of the late 1960s and 1970s.

View from the White Hart.

Ecclesbourne Avenue junction with Town Street.

Wirksworth Road looking towards Hall Farm.

Town Street. The Forge and Town Street seen from Stapleton's upper rooms.

The River Ecclesbourne.

The White Hart, Stapleton's, Jones's.

Tamworth Street and the grounds of
Tamworth House.

The aftermath.

Taking away the rubble. Another view.

Duffield House, The Gables and the White Hart.

(Above and below) Breaking the banks.

Flooding near the Baptist Church.

Memorable snow falls occurred in 1940 and 1947 which remained over a long period. Snow ploughs from the County Council Depot served the village well during these and other lesser falls. Shown here is Hazelwood Road in 1982, of shorter duration but still spectacular.

(Left) Relief Scheme. Recutting near Tamworth House in 1972.

(Below) Preparing for bridge construction on Cockpit Lane.

(*Above*) Tamworth Street. The new bridge. (*Below*) The Green.
New bridge on Snake Lane. The houses behind are on Park Road.

(*Above*) Duffield's Firemen have operated from this station in Snake Lane for more than 70 years. Now, in need of serious attention, it is to be replaced by one on the A6 at Flaxholme, offering easier access and additional up to date facilities. (*Below*) An appliance on display at an event on Gray Recreation Ground. Duffield's first engine was horse drawn.

(Above) A demonstration of equipment. Local firefighters engage in many community and charitable events. (Below) A, fortunately, rare glimpse of the power of the pumps at an event on Eyes Meadow.

Chapter 5 – Youth

In a rural environment there are fewer facilities for youngsters' social life. In a rapidly changing society it is difficult to ensure a safe and secure environment.

For some years there was a youth club associated with the Ecclesbourne School, which eventually closed through lack of support.

Organisations led by the local churches remain popular. Scouts and Guides are well supported. Air Cadets continue.

Cadet Battalion of the Worcester and Sherwood Foresters Regiment

The Duffield Detachment of the Derbyshire Cadet Battalion of the Worcester and Sherwood Foresters Regiment paraded at the Church Hall, Hazelwood Road, for many years. The Battalion enjoyed considerable success in rifle shooting and other sports competing in regional and national events. Annually, in shooting, more than a third of the top hundred cadets nationally were from Derbyshire. Besides annual camps there were some week-end events. The Detachment was absorbed by the Belper C.T.C in 1997.

Duffield Detachment of the Derbyshire Cadet Battalion of the WFR paraded in the church hall, Hazelwood road for many years. The Battalion had considerable success in rifle shooting and athletics with members competing at national level.

The Detachment is shown on Eyes Meadow, *(above)* assisting with the setting up of carnival facilities and, *(left)* with their colours, at their final parade. These had been presented by the Duffield Branch of the Royal British Legion.

The Squadron was formed in 1986 from a Detached Flight of 126 (City of Derby) Squadron. Success has followed in a wide range of activities from aeronautics to shooting plus sporting activity both locally and nationally. Many cadets have participated in the Duke of Edinburgh's Award Scheme and acted as Lord Lieutenant's Cadet.

(Above) Mr Stewart Miller, Managing Director of the Aerospace Group, Rolls-Royce Ltd., talks to Flt. Sgt. Michelle Atkins at the 50th Anniversary of the Air Training Corps Parade in 1991.

(Above) Duffield's Air Cadets at Annual Camp, Coltishall, in 1988. *(Below)* H.Q. Lord Lieutenant of Derbyshire, Lt.Col. Sir Peter Hilton, at the opening of the new H.Q. 1988.

(Above) Flt. Lt. Ian Cowley with past commanding officers of 620 (Duffield and Derby) Squadrons on the 50th anniversary of the A.T.C. *(Below)* Squadron colours being marched through Town Street at a Church Parade to celebrate the 50th Annivery of the A.T.C. February 1991.

(Above) Cadet Tina Hartley firing No.8 .22 rifle. *(Below)* Presentation of WWI Bristol Scout aeroplane propeller, donated by Mrs Winifred Else, through son-in-law and daughter, Mr and Mrs Derek Taulbut.

Youngsters from 6 to 20 take part in a very wide range of activities with Duffield Scouts and Guides. The first Scout section was formed in 1908, the year that the movement was founded. The new centre on Hall Farm Road was opened in 1965.

The Girl Guides have been in Duffield since 1915 (although not continuously). At the Millennium Duffield could boast groups of Beavers (2) Cubs (2), Scouts, Ventures, Brownies (2) and Guides.

(Left) Duffield Scout and Guide centre on Hall Farm Road.

(Below left and right) On the wall-this seems easy!

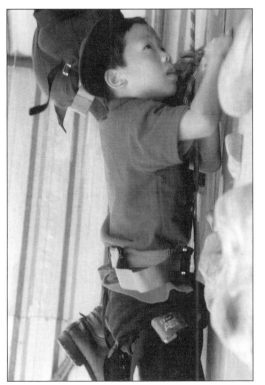

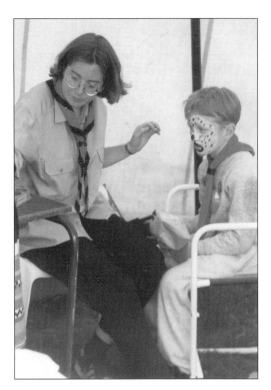 

(Above left) Face painting, for camouflage perhaps. *(Above right)* Eye on the target. *(Below)* On parade in Tamworth Street.

(Above) Award Evening and *(Below)* Presentation.

(Above) Close hauled. *(Below)* The Treck Cart goes to the Carnival.

Learning the ropes and bridge-building.

(Above) Ready for ascent.

(Left) Going Up!

(Above) Rugby Festival at Herbert Strutt. 'A' team in the semi finals.

(Above) Inter School six-a-side football and netball festival, May 1999.

(Above) Douglas McCance and friends 'Mountain Biking', a prize from a skills auction.

(left and below) Two photographs of Duffield Meadow School pupils. Design Project for new Kitchen, 1995.

(Left) Pupils left to right: Sarah Morton; Alistair Dolley; Paul Motteram; Sarah Laizell; Louiae Hogdkins and Jamie Cornish.

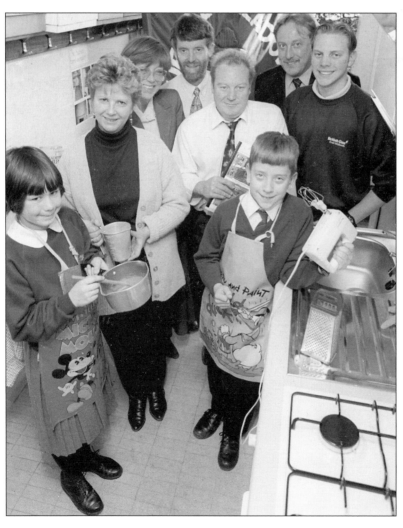

Chapter 6 – Worship and Charity

A notable feature of Duffield, from the 17th century, is acceptance of different faiths and acknowledgement of their places of worship. During the 20th century some, smaller, groups have made use of either peoples' homes or Tamworth House for their meetings.

(Above) St Alkmund's Church. This early view, taken from the Bridge Inn, also shows houses in Church Street.

(Above) St Alkmund's. This interior view dates from the 1880s, a few years before the chancel screen was erected. Note the organ in front of the vestry and two pulpits. *(Below)* The unveiling of the 1914/18 War Memorial in 1921.

(Above) The unveiling of the 1939/45 war memorial tablets on Remembrance Sunday 1947. Shown are Col. Lilley and Sir Ernest Aiton in the foreground.

(Left) A Marriage photograph of Dr William M.Irwin to Mrs Cuthbert Yeomans at Derby Cathedral, 11 September 1933. Dr Irwin was Vicar from 1930-1950.

Church Choir Duffield, circa 1931. 1. George Collyer, 2. Thomas K Bowler, 3. Ivan Wright, 4. Wallace Hearndon, 5. Danny Rhodes, 6. Thomas Degg, 7. Archie Rice, 8. Charles Brighouse – Organist & Choirmaster, 9. Frank Wright, 10. Hector Nelson, 11. Frank Roome, 12. Vernon Smith, 13. Bill Rice, 14. Jack Wheeldon, 15. Paul Collyer, 16. Ainsley Goodwin, 17. Donald Kirk, 18. Anthony Hickling, 19. Keith Ford, 20. Kenneth Stevens, 21. Arthur Fowke, 22. Dr W M Irwin (Vicar), 23. Bernard Wragg, 24. Thomas Wragg, 25. Malcolm McPherson, 26. James Cooper, 27. Harold Burrows, 28. Harold Stone, 29. Donald Day, 30. ?

(Above) Duffield Church Sunday School in the early 1950s, taken prior to one Harvest Festival Sunday. Adults include Rev. George Hatch, Mrs Hatch, James Cooper on the back row with Jack Linfoot (in spectacles, on his left), Miss Margaret Sandham and Miss Joan Lomas.

(Left) St Alkmund's Choir. **Back row:** Geoff Howell; Malcolm Tate; Derrick Smith; Norman Brooks; Kenneth Spruce; David Long and Martin Eades. **Front row:** Rosemary Bull; Pat Brooks, Ann Capel; Heather Sheard; Margaret Eades (conductor and organist); Gwen Radford; Pat Tate; Margaret Tomkins; Marian Taulbut and Anne Smith.

The Rev George Hatch, Vicar 1951-57.

Remembrance Day Service, early 1950s.

Congregation in 1992.

Two fine Church Wardens, *(left)* Ivan Wright and *(right)* Dr James Mason. Both gave many years of devoted service and are commemorated in the new Parish Hall.

Maypole Dancing at the Vicarage Garden Party 1992. The Maypole was also used at William Gilbert's School.

Viewing the New Parish Hall by the church.

(Above) Watching Over Us. This medieval haloed figure is on a beam above the chancel arch. The name was probably of a church warden. *(Below)* Members of the church with Capt. Jeremiah Kashoboorozi of the Church Army in Uganda, linked to the Parish. Left to right are Ann Stanier, Derek Taulbut, Ivy Grocock, Rev. Michael Alexander and John Norreys (1991).

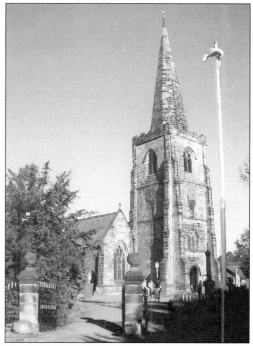

(Above) The retirement of Rev Arthur Geary-Stevens in 1994, photographed by James Bell. Left to right are Rev. Arthur Redman, Richard Lindop and Robin Fugill (both Readers), the Vicar, Mrs Jill Needle and Keith Mantell (both Readers) and Rev. Peter Lyne. *(Above right)* A recent view.

(Left) Duffield Baptist Chapel. When first built it was known as 'The chapel on the Green'. Rerouting of the roads in the last century produced the present layout. A fenced Baptismal site north of Duffield Bridge was associated with it.

(Right) Inside Duffield Baptist Church, preparing for a flower festival.

(Above) Trinity Methodist Church. A Division of the local Methodist movement built these premises which were completed in 1904.

(Left) Emmanuel Community Centre. This chapel was built in 1843 and closed in 1943. It now serves a thriving community.

St Margaret Clitherow

Completed in 1981 (not pictured), St Margaret Clitherow provides a place of worship for Roman Catholics who previously attended masses held at Tamworth House or in Belper.

Several charities were created locally from the 16th century. The buildings of Bradshaws are gone, Potterills have been rebuilt. Others survived to be combined recently into the Duffield Charity.

The Weston Centre offers facilities for the retired of the parish. Annually the Marrieds v Singles football match has raised thousands of pounds for local causes.

The Royal British Legion is a charitable organisation.

Charitable contributions of large sums plus other gifts are made by both individuals and organisa-tions, of which a few examples follow.

(Above) More than a hundred items knitted by Cumberhills W.I. for a Romanian Orphan appeal. Contributions are also made via "Musica in Romania".

Local adventurer Miles Hilton-Barber with guide dog Ivor is shown with pupils from the Ecclesbourne and Meadows Schools. This was a double event handing over money raised from a 'bring and buy' which raised over £200 for 'The Big Take' to aid the street children in Brazil. Emmanuel Community Church was also involved in this.

A cross-country run raised £130 for the R.N.I.B. Miles, who is blind, had run in the London Marathon. Since then his accomplishments include a week-long race in the desert, an amazing walk through Antarctica which nearly reached the South Pole and an ascent of Mt. Kilimanjaro. He has also raised large amounts for the R.N.I.B.

(Right) A Certificate from the National Children's Homes, also to Meadows School.

Certificate
awarded to

THE MEADOWS PRIMARY SCHOOL

in grateful recognition of valued support given to the work of

Barnardos
Together we can give young people a chance.

£332. 84p.

Signed _____ Date July 1998

(Below) The Weston Centre. The R.J.Weston Duffield Charity operates the centre for the daily use of retired residents with morning refreshments and a library. It was completed in 1990.

Besides the original bequest several substantial donations were made by the D.C.A. and Parish Council and others. A number of local groups hire the facilities for regular meetings, including Duffield Art Group, the Debating Group and Gardening Club.

Tamworth House, seen in the rear, is now privately owned.

Augmentations to St Alkmund's from the 1880s had also seen the peal of bells in the tower increased from 6 to 10. Outside Derby at that time it was the only church in the county with this number, and was largely due to Sir Arthur Percival Heywood, an engineer whose home was 'Springwood' on Duffield Bank.

An enthusiastic ringer himself he founded the Central Council of Church Bellringers. He died in 1916 on a visit to Duffield from his home in his later years, Doveleys, at Rocester.

The ringing tradition continues strongly with practices on Tuesday evenings with ringing for Sunday services and other occasions.

The bells were recast in 1933 and dedicated on Saturday 3rd June.

Visit of the Ringers to Boston Stump, with secretary and Church Wardens, summer 1936.

Bellringers in 1960. Standing: John MacArthur; Rev. Martin Boyns; Fred Stone and Arnold Bennett.
Seated: Hilary Mason; Pauline Jennison and Margaret Jervis.

Ready to ring.

Ready to ring, Ronald Bennett; John MacArthur and Fred Stone.

The Bellringers: *(left to right)* Richard Taulbut; Peter Sutton; Gordon Halls; Rev. Arthur Geary-Stevens; David Parkin; A.N. Other; Stephen Irwin.

The Ringers for the 50th Anniversary of V.E.Day.

Royal British Legion

Ex-Servicemen occasionally met in several of the village hostelries until the mid 1930s where more frequent meetings were held at The White Hart (landlord George Sharnwell), and The King's Head (landlord Mason Cockayne), with the Vicar often in attendance. The standard of the Duffield Branch was dedicated on 23rd September, 1938.

An annual dinner was originally held in the 'Boys School'. Tamworth House was purchased in 1945, from which the Duffield Branch operated for many years.

(Left) The house can tell an interesting story. Dating from 1690 several of its owners have leased it rather than lived in it themselves. The double longhouse adjacent to it was built only a few years earlier.

From here the Duffield Branch of the Royal British Legion organised many village activities. Carnivals and other events were later arranged by the Duffield Community Association.

Major Burns leading the Remembrance Day Parade (early 1950s), leaving 'The Green'.

(Above) Presentation to Charles Fry by Maurice Hawley (thought to be a long service award), 1950s. *(Below)* Presentation of Long Service medal to Fred Stone by A.J.Cash. Pictured left to right are the Rev. Martin Boyns, Donald Cash, Vernon Smith, Mr Stone, Maurice Hawley, Col. Marsden and Mrs Adams, the Club Stewardess.

(Above) An Annual Dinner in Tamworth House, early 1950s. At that time the 'Royal' prefix had yet to be granted to the Legion title and (below) after the Dinner.

(Above) Annual Dinner, Women's Section and *(below)* Children's Christmas Party.

(Above) A British Legion Carnival held in the grounds of St Ronan's School. *(Below)* Remembrance Day Service at the War Memorial. In 1997 a memorial stone bearing the names of the fallen of both wars was erected on the Wirksworth Road corner.

Chapter 7 – Refreshment

An 'Enquiry' of 1568 recorded six inns or alehouses in Duffield. Whether any offered service beyond the supply of ale is not stated.

The King's Head accommodated a troop of Parliamentarian soldiers during the Civil War, continuing to serve travellers after that time, including Daniel Defoe.

The White Hart, identified in the 19th century as an hotel, was probably built as a coaching inn for travellers making use of the turnpike roads, with the Wirksworth Turnpike of 1756 being the cause of its transformation from thatched cottage to the Georgian edifice seen through earlier photographs. It had a small forge at the rear for a wheelwright and coach repairs.

The names of a number of early hostelries are known, although their periods of service are uncertain. Besides The King's Head and The White Hart were The New Inn (on Hazelwood Road, known at that time as Wirksworth Road), The Wheatsheaf (which may have been, Phillips Croft), The Castle, The Crown which was demolished to effect the cutting on the Wirksworth branch railway-line, plus its successor The Patten Makers Arms.

The Nag's Head was in Town Street, near the junction with Chapel Street and may be the building now used by the veterinary practice.

The Station adjoined railworkers' cottages enjoying only a short life before conversion into the Station Master's house.

Near the Malt House, on Hall Lane Road (former garage premises and now Church View), stood The Noah's Ark, reputedly popular with farmers and drovers on their way to Derby Markets.

In Church Street stood The White Lion, and finally beside Duffield Bridge stood The Bull's Head which became The Bridge Inn late in the 19th century.

During the 1930s both The White Hart and The Bridge Inn were demolished to make way for the present hostelries.

The Scarsdale was added to the village scene primarily to serve the new housing developments of the 1950s and 1960s.

(*Left*) The King's Head. Until the 1830s the road to the ford across the Derwent, which, via Save Penny Lane, led to Makeney and Holbrook, also a lane to Milford (New Mills Road) passed across this frontage. Note the raised ground level. A major remodelling took place about 1740.

(Above) Patten Makers Arms. Built on the site of a small forge which made the sole plates (pattens) attached to clogs. Adjacent to these extensive premises was the Working Men's Club. *(Below)* The New Inn appears to date from the 1680s. Nearby were scythe stone workings from which many of its early customers were probably drawn. It also served as a resting place for pallbearers on their way to the Parish Church from more outlying parts of the parish.

(Above) The White Hart. Many clubs held meetings here in both the old and new building which dates from the 1930s. *(Below)* King Street. The former Castle Inn stands adjacent to Castle Garden Nursery. The Crown Inn stood near the old school house (demolished 1963) to the left of the picture.

(Above) The Bridge Inn. As The Bull's Head there was a farm here also, and it may have served as toll house for the Chesterfield Turnpike. It was a popular meeting place for hunts and fishermen. (Below) The Lord Scarsdale. Changes and refurbishments are fairly frequent. A major extension was added to the existing public house and the name changed.

Chapter 8 – Associations

At the beginning of the century there were a few organisations using premises in the village for their business, RAOB, Masons, Duffield Club and the Cricket Club for example. Group activity grew diversely as time went on and by the eighties nearly seventy groups were affiliated to the D.C.A. Of some there is no pictorial record, but indications are given here of many of them.

Duffield Club

The Club was founded in 1987 as a private member club to provide recreation and refreshment for its members. It has strong links with Duffield Cricket Club but no political or other affiliations.

The Committee at the Club Centenary 1997. **Back Row:** P.K.Ford; D.Annable; N.G.Storer; F.E.Westmacott. **Middle:** J.D.King; M.K.Blood; W.R.Fretwell; J.D.Street; J.P.Gregory; N.T.Johnson. **Front:** P.G.Cross; F.Browmer; R.de Saeger.

(Right) Duffield Club.

(Below) Dennis Annable in play.

Finals Night party 1996.

First formed in March 1918 the W.I. met in several venues before purchasing the Working Men's Club where their first meetings had been held.

Prizewinners in handicrafts, needlework and produce for many years, they also produced books on cookery and the village itself. With a festival winning choir and a drama group they are also keen quiz contestants.

In the final years of the century their hall, needing extensive repair, was sold and meetings are now held in the Weston Centre.

(Above) Derbyshire Federation W.I. General Knowledge Quiz Final. The Duffield Team, seated, beat Walton (standing, pictured with the Question Master).

(Left) The opening of the Autumn Fair, October 1980, by Mrs Bowles, wife of the Bishop of Derby. (Left to right) Betty Gray, Mrs Bowles and Mrs Cockerham

(Above) Completion of the "Duffield Today" Book in 1965. *(Below)* Grannies Tea. Some of those entertained at an event held annually until 1976.

(Above and below) The Annual Dinner 1974.

(Above) ?, Gwen Yates and Marjorie Mansey at the Autumn Fair 1974. (Below) A scene from the Drama Group presentation of "Hullaballoo".

Duffield Community Association

Duffield Community Association was formed in 1972. Many organisations are affiliated to it covering most of the village activity, helping them as well as having projects of its own.

It also sponsors the local Neighbourhood Watch, carries out plantings and puts up decorations at Christmas and other times.

(Above) Litter Pick, 1972, showing the assembled company before setting out. *(Below)* With the results of their efforts!

(Right) Roy Phillips and Betty Anderson, bulb planting near the library.

(Below) Community Association Workers, Roy Phillips, Betty Anderson, Roy Pooley, Helen Ribbons, ? and Derek Ribbons with bulbs.

(Above) Contestants (left to right) Donald Armstrong; Veronica Byers; Peter Michael and Madelein Barnett in the 'County Quiz' annual competition. *(Below)* Duffield's winning team in 1973, ?, Donald Armstrong, Madelein Barnett, Veronica Byers, Gilbert Orme and Geoff Barnett.

(Above left and right) Village Pump restoration project, near the Pastures. Before and after.

(Right) The Finishing Touch. Restoration of a cast iron milepost by Roy Phillips. This stands on Derby Road near the site of the 'Automatic' and later Kenning Garage - now 'Church View'.

(Above) Raising the Village Flag on Wirksworth Road corner. Left to right, Debbie Knox, James Law, Katie Higgs and Ellie Cooke. *(Below)* Exam success for pupils of the Pamela Smith School of Dance.

(Above) A scene from a show by the school in Derby Guildhall in 1996.
(Below) From the show in 1998.

(Left) Also from the show in 1998.

Duffield Flower Group

Duffield Flower Group was formed in August 1985 at an inaugural meeting held in The White Hart. Their monthly meetings are always well attended and visitors are welcome.

Many members have been associated with church festivals and creation of displays for other events including stately homes.

Royal Crown Derby invited several flower groups to assist in their 250th anniversary celebration with displays which were judged. Duffield's entry was the winner.

Pictured here is the arranger with the President, Programme Secretary, Chairperson and Vice-Chairperson of the group.

Cumberhills W.I. was founded in April 1962, at a time when many new houses were added to the village scene.

The new W.I. met in the evenings while Duffield W.I. met in the afternoons. Its members enjoy a wide field of activity, as shown here.

(Left) Annual Dinner held at Chevin Golf Club. Left to right are Sheila Bentley, Brenda Norreys and Maureen Lodge.

(Below) Carol Dewhurst, Sandra Dare and Yvonne Beadle.

(Above) Annual Dinner held at Chevin Golf Club with Yvonne Beadle, Susie Venkatesh and Ann Capel.
(Below) Pantomime. The Sleeping Beauty.

(Above and below) The Good Old Days. Cumberhills Choir entertain.

(*Above*) Members dispensing refreshment at the 1999 carnival. (*Below and following page*) Cumberhills W.I. entry in the millennium carnival procession, for which they won first prize.

(Above) Left to right are Doreen Suggitt, Avril Parkman, Wilma Shields, Jenny Mills, ?

Following their success at the Millennium Carnival, Cumberhills W.I. were invited to the Crich Tramway Museum to "Demonstrate" (in costume). Pictured Pat Paling, Sandra Dare and Doreen Suggitt.

(Above) Ann Capel, Nan McFarlane and Peggy Evans who assisted in the National Spring Clean 1999.
(Below) Cumberhill walking group visiting Hognaston.

Chapter 9 – Education

Duffield Hall was the home of St Ronan's a private school, from 1919 until 1971. There are many who have happy memories of it. William Gilbert's School served for village youngsters, who, for secondary education, went on to Herbert Strutt School in Belper. The creation of large housing projects brought great changes with a new secondary Grammar school and additional Primary facilities.

William Gilbert's Church of England, Voluntary Aided, School

William Gilbert's School has a long and interesting history. Founded in 1565 on a site between the River Ecclesbourne and The King's Head. It removed to a new site in the 19th century and during the 20th occupied several sites on King Street and Vicarage Lane, on which it has now consolidated.

Willam Gilbert's School. A selection of Middle Infants Form Photographs from 1979/80. *(Above)* Mrs Holloway and Mrs Bonsall, with pupils.

(Above) Pupils with Headmaster HEC (Ted) Weston and Mrs Willetts. *(Below)* Mr Collins' Class.

(Above) Junior Netball Team and (below) Football Team.

Major additions and rebuilding work were completed in 1992 and dedicated by the Lord Bishop of Derby and Lord Lieutenant of Derbyshire. A purpose-built Nursery classroom was added in 1998.

Maplin's at the Village Carnival.

(Above) Old Woman who lived in a Shoe. Preparing for the Village Carnival.
(Below) Three Little Maids from School.

(Above) A Victorian Cameo. *(Below)* School choir at rehearsal.

In Derby Cathedral (Derby Arts Festival).

(Above) Rt. Hon. Kenneth Baker, Minister of Education, with Patrick McLoughlin M.P., Headmaster John Reece, and others.

(Right) Rt. Hon. Kenneth Baker with pupils.

(Left) Demolition of kitchens serving William Gilbert's School, 1989.

Meadows Primary School

Duffield Meadows School was opened in 1965 to serve the growing population having over 300 pupils attending by the early 1980s. Pre-School and Nursery facilities have been added.

"A very effective school", OFSTED Report. A happy group with Headteacher Rex Bleakman.

Hearing about Brazil's Street Children from Ecclesbourne pupils.

Getting involved with "Book Week" 1998.

(Right) Books are Great –
so reads the music being
played by 'Bob the Builder'.

(Below) Storybook
Characters as seen in
Meadows 'Bookweek' 1999.

(Left) 5-a-Side football team with the winners shield, 1988/89.

(Below) Winners in 5-a-Side. Meadows Team in the Belper Schools Section, with two Mayors of Belper and Amber Valley in attendance, 1996.

Winning team in the Duffield Primary (Meadows) School section of the Titterton Football Trophy 1989. Left to right are Simon Bradbury; Chris Dupey; Chris Mills; David Painter; Brett Gerald (holding shield); Philip White; George Walton and Andrew Wood.

Duffield Meadows Primary School Christmas play in St Alkmund's Church.

(Above) Christmas 1995. Scene from "The True Meaning of Christmas" by Class 1.
(Below) "The True Meaning of Christmas". Reception Class.

(Above) A visit by classes 6H and 6T to Elvaston Castle to celebrate 'Christmas Past', 1995.

DERBY ARTS FESTIVAL
COMPETITIVE

DISTINCTION

Class *Mixed Voices Intermediate (Under 12 years)*

Marks *171*

Awarded to

Duffield Meadows School Choir

Date *May 17th 1996*

Adjudicator *David Pollock*

DERBY ARTS FESTIVAL
COMPETITIVE

DISTINCTION

Hymn Singing (Under 12 years)

171

Awarded to

Meadows School Choir

May 17th 1996

David Pollock

This choir won two categories at Derby Arts Festival, Mixed Voices and Hymn Singing in 1996, with Gill Fearn in attendance.

The winning choir in Derby Catherdal for "Mixed Voices, Intermediate";
Derby Arts Festival, 1997.

(Above) Preparing for the Carnival in 1995.

(Left) Duffield pharmacist Peter James, sponsor of the new facilities for the Nursery unit and play group at the opening.

(Above) Some 1998 leavers pictured with Mrs Jean Minion. *(Below)* Remembrance Day 1998.

1998 leavers, ready for Ecclesbourne.

The Ecclesbourne School

Ecclesbourne School opened in September 1957, originally as a County Grammar School. Reorganised in 1976 it became Comprehensive.

It has become very well known as a centre of academic excellence and receives considerable support from parents and the community. This was very evident in the campaign to "Save the VIth Form".

The Entrance in 1985.

(Above) Ecclesbourne School. This view shows the Grammar School, established in 1957, to accommodate 360 pupils from Duffield, Quarndon, Allestree, Darley Abbey and other adjacent villages. Several reorganisations had produced a total number of pupils in excess of 1200 by 1986. Considerable academic success from an early stage in both "O" and "A" levels increased demand for places. An enthusiastic P.T.A. ensured that the school featured very strongly in village life. A school of excellence under only two headmasters, Mr Redfern and Dr J.R.Dupey (who retires this year), it successfully resisted moves to remove its VIth form and constantly seeks greater involvement with the community, having recently attained 'Technology Status'. *(Below)* The Entrance today.

"A" Level Economics group in discussion, 1987.

Computer Studies and I.T.

"A" Level Biology practical workshop.

There were campaigns to prevent the removal of the VIth form from Ecclesbourne School and later becoming Grant Maintained. On both occasions the message was carried to both County Hall and the Mother of Parliaments.

(Above and below) The start of a run to County Hall, Matlock. Part of the "Save the VIth form" campaign with Pauline Latham and Patrick McLoughlin M.P. in attendance.

(Above) Parents and others arriving at Matlock. *(Below)* On the march.

(Above) The crowd assembled outside the County Council Offices. *(Below)* Pauline Latham hands the petition to education vice-chairman, Councillor Sean Stafford. Patrick McLoughlin M.P. also present.

Ecclesbourne upper VIth form May leavers Ball, 1993.

Duffield enjoys music in all its forms. Locally the Derwent Valley Wind Band, with more than sixty playing members, rehearses at the Ecclesbourne School. Concerts for charity are performed several times a year in a variety of venues.

Keyboard and other instrumental skills are taught locally. "Music at Duffield", for the last quarter century, has held seven concerts each year at Ecclesbourne School, but also including some in the parish church.

School concerts are regular events and Derbyshire Building Society has hosted entertainments at Duffield Hall. Both our Primary Schools have award winning choirs and Ecclesbourne School has both choir and orchestra.

Music is often featured in 'pub' offerings and visiting bands play a large part each year in the village carnival.

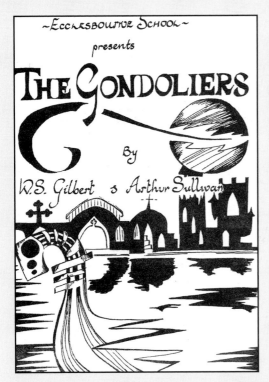 

Ecclesbourne School puts on a variety of entertainment. In the 1980s they performed a series of Gilbert and Sullivan operettas. *(Above left)* The Programme. The last G&S production, 'The Gondoliers', April 1984. *(Above right)* Tim, Derek, Jo and Alison from the cast of 'The Gondoliers', on set for act 2.

(Left) The Programme for Iolanthe, March 1982.

(Left) Josie Hogflesh as an Arcadian Shepherdess and Ward in Chancery, centre is Mark Trimmer as Strephon and Arcadian Shepherd and right is Annabelle Hall as Queen of the Fairies.

Debra Jones as 'Iolanthe'.

Joanna Breknell as 'Leila'.

Peter Taylor as 'The Earl of Mountararat' with
Brian Bonsall as 'Earl Tolloller'.

Julian Haslam as 'The Lord Chancellor'.

(*Above*) Kerry, Fiona and Julia in The Pirates of Penzance. (*Below*) Derwent Valley Wind Band.

The early days of band rehearsals in William Gilbert's School. The band of that time has changed because many of its players leave to go on to higher education. There are always vacancies and frequently two bands, learners and more advanced.

(Above left) Brass at Rehearsal. *(Above right)* The Clarinets. *(Below)* The Band at Alton Towers, July 1995.

(Above) At rehearsal and (below) in concert, with Conductor David Curtiss.

(Above) The band enjoys continental touring and is seen here playing outside the Cathedral Familia Segrada, in Barcelona, 1997. *(Below)* Concert in University Square.

Marching bands in competition, in 1991.

Bands in competition, 1991.

Clubs and individuals are featured here. The village carnival has produced hundreds of images of thousands of people watching or taking part in a wide variety of events. Only a few are shown here to illustrate this delightful festival of entertainment and activity.

Duffield Cricket Club

The village's oldest club is Duffield Cricket Club. Documents confirm its existence from 1878, with a possible record in 1852. 'Battel' and wooden ball games have been known in Derbyshire from the early 17th century. It is unlikely that Duffield would miss out

The Club has used the Eyes Meadow Ground since 1895. Before that games were played in the grounds of Duffield Hall. Located in a most scenic setting the Club continues to gain strength with over sixty playing members at the beginning of the 21st century.

Some of the early club and village characters are shown here. Improvements to ground and club house have helped the Club to maintain high playing standards. The first all-weather pitch in the County (apart from the County Ground) was laid at Duffield.

James Parlby 1851-1939. Club member for 61 years with 37 as a player.

(Above) Duffield Cricket Club in 1900. **Back:** W. Bull; J.Boardman; G.Aldred; H. Hickling; F.Wright; T.Wake. **Middle:** W.Mycroft (umpire); T.Butler; W.Boardman; I.N.Woodiwiss (Capt); J.Parlby; H.H.Mansfield; J.Young; E.Dakin (scorer). **Front:** A.C.Moreton; C.Knifton; G.Green. (Below) In 1921. James Parlby and Toby - attending to the ground. He performed much of the work involved with a little help from other members.

(Above) View of the Ground in the 1920s. (Below) The Team in 1923. **Back row:** J.Parlby; V.I.Wright; H.E.Bowmer; A.Moreton; C.Stiven; K.R.H.Paxton; G.Thornewell. **Front:** ?.Griffiths; W.H.Skinner; E.Shaw; P.White; L.Ashmore. **Scorer:** H.Hickling.

(Above) The 1st XI in 1946. **Back row:** E.Butterworth; G.T.Cutts; J.W.Hoyle; H.H.Webb; G.C.Glover; K.J.A.Coley. **Front:** W.Cooper; C.C.Mellor; F.Johnson; L.H.Coley; V.I.Wright. *(Below)* The Annual Dinner at the White Hart on January 26, 1951.

(Above) The Annual Dinner at The White Hart on January 26, 1951 and *(below)* in 1952.

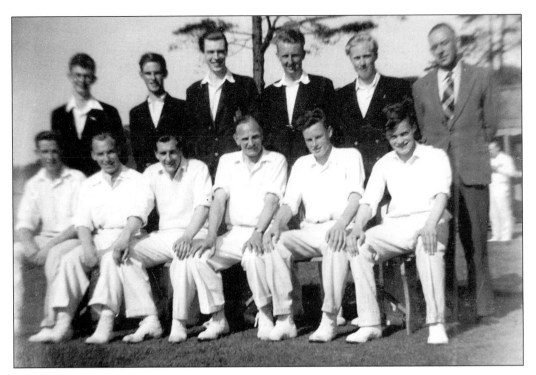

(Above) The Team of 1955. **Back:** D.Gilman; J.P.Bennett; K.V.Gregory; L.F.Smith; G.Bell; C.C.Mellor. **Front:** G.Warrington; W.E.Hudson; J.R.Blackton; K.J.A.Coley; I.C.B.Spriggs; D Spriggs. *(Below)* At the Annual Dinner of 1956. **Standing:** Mrs L.H.Coley; Mrs Fredu Brown; Billy Oates (Allestree C.C.); Harold Pepper (Belper Meadows C.C.); K.V. Gregory; R.Masser and L.F.Smith. **Seated:** Will Taylor (Secretary Derbyshire C.C.C.); F.O.Dann; Mrs Crook; L.A. Crook (President Duffield C.C.); Mrs E.Coley and K.J.A.Coley.

(Above) A Sunday XI in1962. **Standing:** G.T. Copestake; A.P.Turner; K.V. Gregory; J.E.Horton and D.W.G.Smith. **Seated:** M.C.Stilliard; K.J.A.Coley; H.W.Lomas; R.Bennett; J.P.Bennett and J.I.Goatham. *(Below)* First XI v Melbourne Town, 1966. **Back row:** P.Bennett; R.Jones; I.C.B Spriggs; B.G.Lucas and F.Hudson (Umpire). **2nd Row:** G.Warrington; M.E. Riley; J.E.Horton; E.J.G Orme and W.E.Hudson; **Front Row:** ?; R.K.Exley.

(Right) The opening of the pavilion extensions in June 1971. Ken Coley performed the opening watched by Ken Gregory and Jeff Goatham.

(Above) The Junior XI, 1977. **Back row:** J.P.Bennett (coach); A.Coope; M.Bull; A.Raw; P.Crisp; S.Coope and S.Illingworth. **Front row:** M.Parker; T.Salt; N.D.Thorn; S.G. Torn (captain); P.Molyneux; M.Weston and J.Mason.

Ken Coley's XI 1978. **Standing:** G.T.Cutts (umpire); J.P.Bennett; R.Jones; G.Warrington; A.P.Turner; D.Holland; A.A.Cross; D.S.Thorn and C.C.Mellor (umpire). **Seated:** L.F.Smith; F.R.Smith; K.J.A.Coley; K.V.Gregory; R.Masser and ?

The 2nd XI 1985. **Standing:** I.Goodwin; P.Crisp; M.Roberts; A.Walker; D.Stone and P.Nolan.
Front row: R.Hedway; J.C.Rowlands; K.Mcloughlin; N.McLoughlin and J.Cunliffe.

Carnival Match 1990. For many years Carnivals were organised by the Duffield Branch of the Royal British Legion from Tamworth House.

A Garden Party in the 1920s. These ladies were obviously accustomed to such events.

Duffield Bowls Club (at Milford) 1982.

Bowls match at Broom Park 1923

The Club celebrated its centenary in 1994. The course must surely be among the most scenic to be played on anywhere.

Starting with a course of 9 holes in 1984 it was increased to 12 in 1905 and a year later to the full 18. It was laid out on land originally owned by the Strutt family and George Herbert Strutt was the first of the club's six presidents to date.

With a membership of more than 800, the majority living in Duffield, there is also a thriving junior section.

With excellent amenities for members at the 19th hole the club is proud of its interactive associations with the surrounding community.

(Above) View of the front of the clubhouse from Golf Lane showing the practice putting green and 1st tee, looking towards the Chevin. *(Below)* Clubhouse interior.

(Above) Clubhouse interior. *(Below)* Centenary Captain Michael Riley presents Club President John Flanders with his red jacket, in recognition of being President of the English Golf Union for 2000.

Charity Golf Tournament. The Duke of Devonshire, Patron of the Tiny Tim Charity, is seen here with officials of the Charity and the Club, 1999.

(Left) Club Captain Ron Scullion driving off on January 1st 2002, watched by more than 150 club members. This drive went "straight down the middle".

(Above) W.I.members enjoying a game of croquet.

(Above) Great facilities at Duffield Tennis Club. Duffield's second oldest club, founded in 1882, is the oldest tennis club in the Midlands. Since that time they have occupied virtually the same site.

More than forty years ago the club built the first squash court, forming the basis of the Squash Club. Both clubs share the premises, but operate independently. Plans are in hand for a major redevelopment to move the clubs closer to being a joint Sports Club. There are over 440 members using 7 artificial courts, 3 of them floodlit. There are 17 senior teams and 6 junior, with many members playing at County level. The Club has 2 professional coaches. It also offers community tennis to newcomers on Sunday evenings.

(Above) Duvelle Bowmen with their founder, retired teacher Bev Johnson (6th from the left). Field Archery is often shot instinctively at marks of anything from 10 to 180 yards, here *(Below)* they are shooting at a mark of approximately 140 yards distance.

(Above and left)
Carnival Queens and
their entourages.

The events eventually
ceased. They were
revived in 1975 by the
Duffield Community
Association.

(Above and above left) Carnival Queens and their entourages, late 1950s.

(Above) Celebrity television gardener Dr Stefan Buczacki opening the Christmas fair in 1992.

A young Captain Hook ready for an early sixties carnival.

(Above and below) Part of the Carnival Procession in 1991.

(Above) Willi Gilli Carnival Float. *(Below)* Carnival princess travels by carriage.

(Above) Part of the Carnival Procession in 1991. *(Below)* Carnival Princess in open tourer.

(Above and below) Local businesses are very generous with help for the village carnival. Seen here are vehicles of Hawley Colour Works and Faulkners Duffield Transport being prepared for use by the British Legion and Meadows School.

(*Above*) Carnival Princess – open tourer. (*Below*) Chitty Chitty Bang Bang.

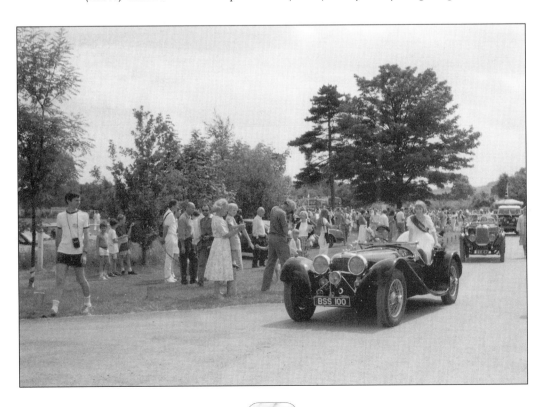

(Above) Winning float for 1989. (Below) Keith Stocks Chairman of Duffield Parish Council, Eyes Meadow.

(Above) Derek Cook (D.C.A. Secretary) and Maureen Cook enjoying the events on Eyes Meadow. A happy group. *(Below)* Tug-o-war, or having it both ways at once!

Chapter 12 – Millennium

The Millennium was celebrated in many ways. An early project was for the Millennium Meadow where 14 acres of Eyes Meadow would be dedicated to a restoration trust, with native species which would also restore wildlife and vegetation which has disappeared.

Millennium Meadow. The proposed area.

Pupils from Meadows School planting in July 2000.

(Above) Rosie Hackland, Carnival Princess, presenting the prize for best float design to Cumberhills.
(Below) Ecclesbourne School's Millennium Clock.

(Above) Chairman of Duffield Parish Council, Richard Knibbs and Alan Stewart, Chairman of Duffield Community Association, assist the Millennium Carnival Princess and attendants, to bury the Time Capsule on Wirksworth Road corner. *(Below)* The Millennium Signpost with plaque in place.

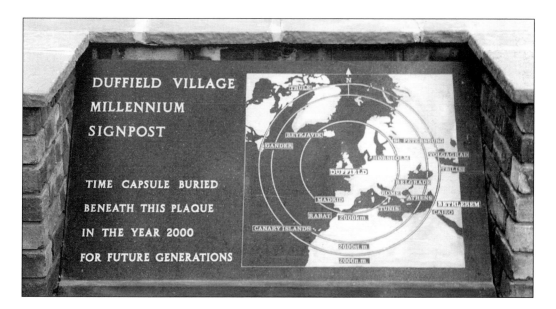

The Amber Valley Millennium Project produced eighteen banners in total, illustrating aspects of life and locations within the area. It began in Duffield with planning discussion in December 1999 with work starting in January 2000, much of it carried out in the Weston Centre.

Members of Cumberhills and Duffield Women's Institutes, and friends, combined to ensure the success of the artwork.

Duffield's theme represents places by picture and activity by motif, showing scenes and ideograms of the many activities that take place within the village.

The textile banner, with sides a metre long, was exhibited in a variety of locations in Amber Valley, including Alfreton Hall and also the Houses of Parliament, attracting much comment and praise, finally returning to Duffield.

(Above and below) Details of the Millennium Banner.